REALLY NOT REALLY

Fee Griffin is a writer from the east coast of England. Her debut poetry collection, *For Work/For TV*, won the Amsterdam Open Book Prize and was published by Versal Editions in 2020. She works at the University of Lincoln with some amazing colleagues and students, whose work inspires her. She rides a beautiful orange wheelchair at obnoxiously high speed and lives with her husband, four children and a dog from the Carpathian Mountains. She likes them all very much.

Praise for *Really Not Really*

After *For Work/For TV* – her extraordinary debut collection and dazzling love letter to the kings and queens of factory canteens, workshops, and bus stops – Griffin continues her interrogations of life's delicate structures with formal agility, tonal virtuosity, and imagistic subtlety. In *Really Not Really*, her second collection, she proves yet again her ability to capture the unremarkable as a reminder of our need for constant reflection and (re)discovery of not only ourselves, but the realities that shape our lives. And when she writes that no matter how "long the world lasts / it is better to have three mushrooms than two," she doesn't write as a poet – she writes as a philosopher, a magician, and a sage. In short, Griffin has a voice, imagination, and linguistic dexterity like no other poet writing today, and *Really Not Really* is simply a brilliant sophomore collection by a poet who shines on and off the page.

— Daniele Pantano, *Home for Difficult Children*

To read *Really Not Really* is to climb inside the body of someone who sees and feels the world in all of its kaleidoscopic disparity, its bizarre and surreal absurdness. And yet this collection of beautifully crafted poems makes complete sense. Sense, in the way it calls into question our daily lives, the HOW! HOW! HOW! of our strange existence. Every sentence is another layer of earth giving way beneath our feet, every page a Pandora's box begging to opened. As we fall down the rabbit hole we practice funerals, drive in haunted cars, stand aghast at the size of the ocean. This is poetry that uncovers the hidden, of internal human anxiety, the crushing external weight of our mortality. And yet to say all this is really an injustice at the brilliance of Griffin's observations , and this exceptional book is much much more than can adequately be explained in just three simple dimensions.

— Stuart McPherson, *End Ceremonies*

Fee Griffin's *Really Not Really* is a breakneck descent into wry wit. These poems are fresh and full zesty surrealism, written in a voice that is lively and engaging, treats you like a confidante, tells you tall tales you are too charmed to not believe.

— Cathleen Allyn Conway, *Bloofer*

Really Not Really

Fee Griffin

Broken Sleep Books

Also by Fee Griffin

For Work/For TV   (Versal Editions, 2020)

For anyone who was ever not sure
which bit of reality was real
at the time

ISBN: 978-1-915760-42-5

Cover designed by Aaron Kent

Edited and Typeset by Aaron Kent

Broken Sleep Books Ltd
Rhydwen
Talgarreg
Ceredigion
SA44 4HB

Broken Sleep Books Ltd
Fair View
St Georges Road
Cornwall
PL26 7YH

Contents

When I Was a Hammerhead Shark 11

Just before you go, your hand still on the door— 12

How/ How/ How (I) 13

What Keeps Me Going Is 14

Unusable Tarot Reading from the Passenger Seat [...] 16

Inscription in an Austin A55 mk 2 / Austin A60 Workshop Manual 17

Carotid Artery I Can Hear the Sea 18

People Just Add Something; This Time the Thing Is a Mole 19

Fossdyke and the Native Speed of Birds 20

Call for Help 22

HELLO MY NAME IS 23

Futility of Trying to Enter a 240-Year-Old Public House from Orbit 24

Palm Pocket Palm 26

How/ How/ How (II) 27

How/ How/ How (III) 28

You Do Know 29

Soaking the Labels off the Jars 32

Azaleas Make a Comeback 33

Bruegel Crowd Depicting the Top Ten News Stories Online 34

Following Advice to Be Myself at a Party [with subtitles] 35

During or After a Party   36

How/ How/ How (IV)   37

How/ How/ How (V)   38

Reliable Witnesses   39

In Which a Council Employee Swears She Sees Mothman [...]   40

LUCKY NUMBERS   41

In the conversation about who dies first you imagine   42

Love Poem During Which I Invent the Electric Kettle   43

Maxim Asks the Man   47

Search History   48

Jessica DMs Me a Photograph of Badly Decorated Eggs at Easter   49

Haiku from the other side of the road   50

When the Translator Is Grieving   51

Neil told me   54

When Lindsay Denton from BBC TV Show Line of Duty [...]   55

On Becoming Unwell After Reading a Biography of Richard III   58

This Recovery Doesn't Fit   60

Partial Biography with Chital Deer   61

There Was a Woman Who   62

Diatomite or Diatomaceous Earth or Moler Earth or Kieselguhr   63

If Something Has Fallen into the Box by Mistake [...]   65

Acknowledgements   69

When I Was a Hammerhead Shark

I was always knocking my eyes on the sides of kitchen units. People would laugh. By chance we moved to an old town where a lot of the buildings had the corners cut off for cartwheels. That helped. In my first job interview in the new town the lady said *I CAN SEE FROM WHAT YOU'RE WEARING THAT YOU'RE NOT VERY INTERESTED IN FASHION AND TO BE HONEST I WOULD HAVE EXPECTED TO SEE A BIT OF MAKEUP.* I walked out. The coat hangers worried me anyway. Mostly I just got dinner ready, went to work, whatever. This lasted about twenty-five years. I loved how you thought I was smiling at you the whole time.

Just before you go, your hand still on the door—

No, you say, Count Duckula was a vegetarian, that's why they
filled him up with ketchup instead of blood when they resurrected him.
Really? I ask but I no longer know what I mean by that.

How   you learned the Latin for *What year is it* and *Who is the Prime Minister* to no avail or at least no obvious avail or at least no profit

How   sometimes we made illustrations about the future but when we got here we found out it was the wrong one and left unsatisfied

How   you dismissed photographs as single-use mirrors

What Keeps Me Going Is

I carry a photograph of Patti Smith in my lungs   this photograph
      is one cell thick like the walls of blood capillaries and has
a large
surface area
like prison walls do

                                    from the outside

I am careful not to breathe on Patti Smith

                               I sing on
short car journeys so the image of her eyes can see out of me and of Patti
Smith this photograph which is
          of Patti Smith diffuses from a high concentration in my lungs to a
lower concentration in my red blood cells   this is how
substances move around our bodies

the presence of
this photograph

(of Patti Smith)   betrays my childish idea of
                the lungs as empty & operating like bagpipes
in reality
of course
my tissues are fused with the Kodak paper

         I have been
unable to do well since January a

                        pale absence forms
over areas of Patti Smith like she's been play-
ing

Earth Angel to her young parents in a hall under the Atlantic that's
wrong you say and each time I say *it's spring* you correct me to *late spring* my
heart compensates
　　　by beating
　　　too fast　my arms shake when I eat
　　　　　　　　　　　　　　　　this chest x-ray

is two weeks old but I have not been called back
by the doctor who delays
　　　　　and delays struggling to form her question—

Unusable Tarot Reading from the Passenger Seat of a Crashed Peugeot 205 (1997)

So my friend kisses a horse on the horse's
face, breaks it to me gently that my car is
haunted, cuts the deck. We drive to the
seaside. Around us puddles cough up spits
of oil, slips of clay, root stock, rock salt, this
sky rains *the business*. This guy will get out
of his car, she predicts, like early morning
children's TV, give up memories of a pond
he can't place, of car chases and crows.
There'll be a grease-green 90s toaster
smashed and abandoned at an angle in a
skip, elements like fake limbs in a reclined
seat. There'll be a parting in the loosened
area of reeds around the windshield, and
we'll find ourselves outstretched on the
tarmac, if not with the impact then with
madness at how the sea can take a place
over, behind and around your attention,
grind the sharpness from glass, the ink
from your eye. The nightless wonder of the
unorbited, the outbid. Tassels from denim.
Plastic from sand. Lean on the wing mirror
with me a minute, OK? Did I tell you how
big the sea has got?

Inscription in an Austin A55 mk 2 /
Austin A60 Workshop Manual

The illustrations, line drawings, are more beautiful than is required.
I am sure that the makers of the Austin A55 mk 2 (1958–61)
and the Austin A60 (1967–69) had hope
that you would feel the same about your car.
I note that you ran your A55 Cambridge model (1959)
to Reading, from Billericay, with no oil.
I am not surprised you heard the sounds you so vividly describe
in the coming months, or at least,
the months that were still to come in the final days of 1974.
Your signature, beneath the paragraph, had not yet reached
its final form, while you had so recently taken yours.
Seeing it now is like watching Series 1, Episode 1
of something long running and popular:
Lisa's hair is the wrong shape,
Bart's eyes are too far apart,
and everyone is the wrong shade of yellow.
I do not know how you felt about your car; whether the
beauty of the illustrations provided by Kenneth Ball G I Mech E and the
Autopress Team of Technical Writers
seemed to you to do justice to the innermost parts
of your A55 Cambridge model. I only know that the reason
for the thudding became apparent as you took the head off:
one of the cylinder bores was completely
full of water.

Carotid Artery I Can Hear the Sea

I never saw it written down,
only heard it in Silent
Witness during an autopsy. I
imagined it a thing having
happened, heard 'carotted'
like 'garrotted,' 'corrected'
or 'corroded'; a cause of
death a mistake a
contributing factor not just a
part, named. A teacher, later,
corrected a title to capitalise
the 'I' of 'is'; I hadn't known
that 'is' was a verb, that just
being, now, was enough to
qualify as an action. You're
doing it right now, oxygen-
rich blood passing this verb
unchallenged into your head,
face, brain. Feel them, call it
sound if you like: The paths
of two narrow
misunderstandings either side
of a windpipe.

People Just Add Something;
This Time the Thing Is a Mole

I went to Enid's funeral and there was a mole on the coffin and it seemed aware of us but unconcerned. Also—and not to underplay this—the seats were made of moles and everyone there was a mole. After, I shook their clawed hands as best I could and they said Fee you are the great-niece who is always talking about moles! It struck me as odd how earlier they must have paid someone to dig the big hole with spades.

Now around six months later all the mole hills fall flat at once, bespoke sinkholes calculated perfectly by a podium of child geniuses. I think of Debbie and her daughter calling to one another on the eventless, minimally reactive surface of the earth, low VOCs. Things are repainted. The moles have all gone. Maxim walks the new flatness complaining how in films the gravestone is always erected too soon.

Fossdyke and the Native Speed of Birds

We hit on something by mistakenly playing 45 vinyl at 78 speed
while my father burned his finger with bleach in the kitchen.
Geological time one speed, Godspeed another, and then the birds. The times of
trees of brambles hurried up for Attenborough, the time my brother and I used nail
scissors to hollow out a hedge, crept inside and watched the birds play the
33 grass breeze at 78, sparrows sudden about the place like waking to a noise or
falling. You see that? said my dad, that's my skin boiling away. Like chalk seams
the water sees, sinkholes all over Norwich, buses taken into the hill.
The weight of a glacier would have pushed the land down here, closer to sea level.
You won't damage it by playing it at the wrong speed, but you will if you
use the wrong kind of needle, causing high flows on the River Trent
after the construction of the lock at Torksey. It's tempting to do the same
with time when you see it come up out of the ground like that:
let it bunch and gather regardless of the building drop, colluvium and peat.
A Roman throws a statue in, a Georgian gets out again;
the most disjointed conversation in history. My brother left;
we crossed the Thorne Waste to look for him in parts of Doncaster
whose paleochannels gather water named as pools.
I read it in a PDF of a habitat plan.
We drove round old battle sites and pavements while birds scattered, a few
gathering in air-buried channels where more had been before;
maps written in lemon juice, a pencil leaded with the magnetism of the Earth.
My brother had painted his room black before he left; I didn't see him
for maybe a year after that. In the satellite image, the thick blue band running
through the page is my sense of nostalgia.
It's possible I've been trying not to think of this for longer, of the pawned
VCR player and paleochannels, older versions of the way to the sea.
That time when North Sea ice blocked the outflow and laked it all across
the Humber. I could drive you to a hill that used to be a cliff,

still too steep in places for me to climb. All these seabed houses pushed
down by the 33 grass breeze waiting for it at a speed
native to horsehair plaster, those blue outlines and planning permissions.
There's ditchy drains, water parsnips, notes about ground elevation;
this Bronze Statuette of Mars just hanging around at the native speed of bronze.
I never found out why my dad did that to his finger, other than to
demonstrate to my friend and I what would happen.
The rest of his hand went to smoke, not earth in the end, sediment settling
in the old lines of air left by native birds.
Me and my friend were there both times he boiled away into space.
I knew a road in Germany called Unter dem Himmel which translates as
under the sky, and when you look up you can imagine the surface of the sea
above you quite easily in the cloud layer; it's all the same.
You should stand very still while the channel moves progressively
south-west towards you over hundreds of years.
You should play Jolene by Dolly Parton at 33 instead of 45; it sounds just fine
and is still too high in places for me to reach.

Call for Help

After lying down amongst the string and rubber stamps
or whatever is to hand
and sleeping the cool long line between Fridays
I remembered there's a phone number you can call
to hear a glacier melting in real time
from anywhere in the world
which by coincidence
is where I was at the time.
I tried to call the melting glacier but
found the glacier had been disconnected in 2008
and my doctor's engaged tone was dripping
endlessly that half hour into
Jökulsárlón lagoon.

HELLO MY NAME IS

I have placed a security tag on my sense of loss and every time I try to leave the building with it an alarm sounds, and a lot of security guards rush to apprehend me. If you're not sure if this is melancholy or exciting, let me tell you: it is exciting. This has no special ending: I just stay home with the guards, offer them tea, ask them where they got their jackets.

Futility of Trying to Enter a 240-Year-Old Public House from Orbit

The moon starts with the usual sort of thing, in
& out being the most popular gesture of all time:

> object permanence
> another person's body
> shade & light
> those are the main ones
> not forgetting
> the hokey-cokey

Long time it sends its light or, with professional
distance, the light of another into this 240-year-
old building in a small town it met one night
near the head of a new canal.

> *Notes on dog behaviour: There are assumptions made by a dog of the
> postman's intentions towards the 240-year-old building. The dog barks
> to prevent the postman entering through the letterbox. This proves so
> successful, the dog does it every time.*

The collie who lives in the 240-year-old building suspects
the satellite of collusion with the Post Office, despite scant
evidence of the postman ever having been to the moon &
even though the moon is considerably older than the postman:

> his gloved hand
> the Post Office itself
> the evolution of dogs

Notes on satellite behaviour: Its sunlight is older than your sunlight. It was happiest the night Pompeii turned to stone & it could broadcast light from its silent rock onto the silent rocks of humans formed. Its favourite animal is those bald cats.

Occasionally a dog puts two & two together & gets
238 thousand miles, figures out that yes: the moon
would like to enter the 240-year-old-building. This
realisation is what you are hearing when dogs bark
outside at night.

> The moon shuts this right down
> That is why there are dog statues

The Collie does not enter the garden but barks from the
safety of the lounge bar. Out of exasperation the publican
leaves the curtains open every night for a year, a sort of
aversion therapy for the dog. The neighbours vacate after
5 weeks. The dog feels powerful on this account & also
on cloudy nights but even during its *threat phase* the moon
still moves away from the 240-year-old building at a rate
of 4 cm per year —

> despite its ongoing & tragic enactment
> of the most popular gesture of all time

Palm Pocket Palm

I am walking this spaniel, a
creature bred for anticipation.
He is waiting at all times for
me to turn to him. He expects
at all times there to be a ball in
my pocket. This is not the case.
To indicate no ball I make a
gesture of open flat palms the
way Jesus does in those pictures
of blessings or maybe when
he's just thinking *oh wow* or
has sticky fingers and doesn't
want them to touch. I heard
somewhere that 'now' is just
our best guess of what's about
to come true anyway. Some-
times it comes false instead
and that is called mental illness.
I'm not saying I think 'no ball'
was the original message, the
one people went crazy for. But
who knows? Sports have always
been very popular. Jesus sighs,
answers slowly on the sports
field, over the fence, to a span-
iel on a canal path: *I don't have
your ball.* The creatures bred for
anticipation turn eagerly, look
from palm to pocket to palm.
So there *is* a ball.

How   you touch me: each one of my blood cells is shaped
like a 1980s graphic of a palm tree against a sunset

How   Leonard Cohen pretending to be Kris Kristofferson
in a 1970s hotel lift is a sexual orientation all by itself

How   we spent so many afternoons in kitsch vest tops on
rooftops guessing the R value of *I love you*

How   Marks & Spencer's is on fire these days
                and the card shop is on fire too

How   if you cut me right now I would bleed
                pterodactyls all over these carpet tiles

How   *well* everyone says the haunting is going!

You Do Know

(Three Unrelated Fires)

Gershon said, before he was ordained, that
if there were no Jewish people, there would
be no Jewish G-d. We followed as far as *if
there was no more planet Earth*, talked a
while in that jointly brought about void
about Vonnegut, toyed with those three stars
of Orion's—or anyone's—belt from another
perspective being just three unrelated fires.

1. Alnilam, around 1,975.8 light
   years from here winds blowing fast
   around the fire, dropping mass fast
   & I mean like 20 million times
   faster than the sun. Hoods up.

You do know you can't really touch another
Person—a geographer called Josephine told
me on a fold-out chair during a presentation
about pollution in a local river, I was so
relieved. The electrons in your fingers repel
the electrons of the intended touched. Third
party, I will keep all your emails titled (for
example) *Re:* ██████████████████
████████████████████

2. Alnitak is preoccupied with
   league tables, all 5th brightest star
   in Orion & joint 31st of the whole
   sky. I haven't got time for it.

Member of a number of trade associations, all on fire, such as the Orion OB1 association (subgroup OB1b) & the Collinder 70 open cluster (so much fire).

Monday & I'm cleaning the big house on Westgate. All around me electrons interact with each other by exchanging photons. The momentum of both is changed, pushes them back apart. I touch their piano with my cloth, which does not quite happen, but still the embarrassment of them listening to me clean the open keys, workday jazz accidental. I change their sheets. They never touch. It's so personal. All around me their square footage proposes a completely redundant second distance between all of their possessions. The wealthy don't trust electrons *at all*.

3. Mintaka Aa1 & Aa2 orbit each other, it takes 5.73 days. There are slight variations in the brightness as they eclipse one another, over & over, round & round, speaking fire to fire. The nerve of it.

Everything in my house is closer, but none of it is touching. When you email me, photons come flying right out of my computer screen. When I see you, we exchange force-carrying particles, which is touching but unsentimental.

Your belt, which I have not thought about, is
pinholes in leather; hold it up to the window
& eclipse of an unrelated fire can be safely seen
with only our naked eyes as a surface to fall on.

Soaking the Labels off the Jars

The trope is two men walk away from an explosion. Bob Ross looks mildly
at a snowscene, the feel is ASMR. I put my finger in a jar of tap-cold water
and think of you. Georgie says it's because you want him to make you feel
something.

Azaleas Make a Comeback

By the early light of the flat east you swear to me that Caroline Quentin owns Wyevale Garden Centres / hysterical with incredulity that anyone wouldn't believe this unclassified truth / I slam the windscreen wipers on with all the force of a sharp left in a car you're not used to driving and pass the entrance as Caroline must / with speed / impossible as it is to maintain facts as untethered as these / even if you are a trained actor / even paid above Equity rates / to act out the great administrative burden / of another person's delight

Bruegel Crowd Depicting the Top Ten News Stories Online

People are practicing funerals, sequestering ocean liners, pleading for hysterectomies under the arch. People are bagging lottery prizes after mishaps with their glasses, suing TV doctors for defamation in fields of wheat. People are jailed for audacious supermarket robberies at the well bucket, queuing untenably for aeroplanes on unsuitable ladders. People are dying disgraced financiers in small-windowed rooms. People are begged by office managers for their lives upon enormous barrels of unknown contents. People are waking from their sleep and slashing prices in blousy white linen under tree shade. Photographs are credited to bystanders.

Following Advice to Be Myself at a Party
[with subtitles]

Everywhere as we left
people had realistic
faces and necks
like a luxury zombie movie with
a high affinity to solid matter.
Tell me what you want, I said,
using only physical objects and no
latent ideas floating to the top riding a
zinc chloride solution. There are
microplastics in my decision-making process
and my ability to recognise faces is
waking up with hot legs from sleeping in trousers not
thinking of Laura Prepon and
old firework casings unfurling during spring like
premixed croissant tubes warming on the polycarbonate roof
and how when crying over loss my
mouth opens wider and wider my neck opening and
also my chest
all of which are realistic. Don't
mistake me I'm not
solemn about this; please let's think
quickly about the sound of a dog eating crisps on the Internet.
[Indistinct chatter] is my favourite closed caption subtitle and
YES
I need a text description of what I am hearing
so I can fail the Turing test and
still join in, indistinctly, with my realistic face and neck.

During or After a Party

It is compassionate to tell a website that you understand and accept
It is lucid to hold a cereal box like the Virgin Mary
It is friendly to raise your hand to a taxi but never   strike
It is inexhaustible to drive to the next town in no jewellery
It is inelegant to press cut but never paste
It is inadvisable to inform the old men dressed as wasps that they are out of copyright
It is honest   look at me like cold tap condensation, all outside itself
It is dormant to move the correspondence to a lower drawer
It is ambiguous to demonstrate how to lie properly on   couch
It is futile to issue a summons for   during or after a party
It is   to miss things said because your head is underwater
    is disturbing to   the sounds the Internet made when it was young
It is against house rules   tattoo of a tiger on the chest
It is glib to   the smell of houses with   smallest profitable rooms
    is bankrupt to   and then say 'fact'
It is   to   cough and   on the window seat
        hurried   or to break before
                        and then   twice
    is a
It   without
        contradiction to
                                empty the only water
    is without   what
It
    is

How   when you notice the sun rises every day,
                 you think of the understudy

How   you start seeing understudies everywhere
                 after that

How   the hedge stands by, waiting for the gate
                 to sicken

How   I say I have a conscience, but you've seen it
            and it's a prosthetic

How   you knelt down in front of me to plug in
            your phone by my foot

How   I did not feel very heterosexual about that
            at all

Reliable Witnesses

After the ancient Roman sculpture of Pan and the nanny goat (in marble)

I used to know this guy who claimed
                              convincingly
on a night out
that in an unaccounted few moments
                              on a small street
the Greek god Pan came to him and said

                    don't be such a bloody idiot

but Pan (who has sex with goats while
          Paparazzi sculptors chip on)
                              can't talk

while being a great role model and
                    (look at it going in)
a great nude model
and a goatfucker and
                    very possibly
someone's idea of a bloody idiot.

I wonder if he was *intimidated*
I wonder what happened to that guy I knew,
if he:

          moved away or
          took up with sculptors or
          kept on in the admin job —

In Which a Council Employee Swears She Sees Mothman at the End of Skegness Pier

The moon loves an app: shines with the sun, throws with the sea. Shells & sailor bones smooth glass blue chip fork fragments descending stones. The landmasses are 10/10 embarrassed: all that rubbing things together. She's got HOT FRESH DONUT fatigue those deckchair blazers of 1970s Wrates photographers, telescopes instructing DON'T LOOK AT THE SUN & that privately owned sentiment: you've got 20p & Skegness sees you.

When the moon laughs there's an eclipse & all the manhole covers on North Parade take on ritual significance. The moon loves it when people say *a stone's throw from here*. A man asks directions, adds that this is *really no better than Hunstanton pier*. The moon's throw comes up out of the ocean like bleeding knees, better than the top ten knife throwers in Skegness, ranked; better than all the javelin throwers in a flat county; better than all the brightly painted wood in the world, revolving.

Skegness beach breaches: all that brightly painted wood & wire, stock photo Monroe, Pirate & Wild River rides brace. Two roads back a cast iron butterfly lands on a roof & there it is — sat on the pier — awful with large black wings, fish & chips underfoot & those big glasses like Elton John wore all those years, 7ft tall & HOT FRESH DONUTS floating past like too much, like way too much, like the tide comes into a sweet shop & asks the fiftieth time for your number.

LUCKY NUMBERS

It's incredible what you can do without, he says to the unicorn, spilling a little of his drink, listing *tax breaks, temperatures in the mid-twenties, speedboats, branded breakfast cereals, The White Stuff catalogue, pre-grated cheese, a twenty-year collection of herbs and spices, complimentary tickets, the good will of mid-career TV hosts, paved front steps, elaborate explanations for simple problems, those little porch lights with their own roof*—

In the conversation about who dies first you imagine

two men dressed like Elvis at your funeral
but neither of them sing
OK, OK,
OK,
imagine a thirteenth century king playing a Hammond organ
on a school stage
then coming
directly
towards you—that kind of vibe only

imagine
the movement of the smoke in the chimney at the moment
the chimney is falling
(then run)

imagine loving light so much you suck it all inside you
(then cleaning your teeth with blackboard paint)

imagine arranging a buffet,
phone between jaw and shoulder,
the kind of soft panic that rises like
salt and vinegar crisps on the wet ringing membrane
of the inside of your lip, imagine

the two Elvises bonding over vol-au-vents, comparing diaries, embracing, even.

imagine taking six garlic capsules a day and still
introducing so many kings.

Love Poem During Which I Invent the Electric Kettle

1

Carefully I
plug in then unplug an electrical fan or say I do
wonder at the blades' faithfulness to one another, the chase lacking in variation like
the heart (my Fitbit says I am doing quite well though I have been watching
old health shows from the 00's
and learn that
a man wearing the same shirt as you has died recently).
I dream that Gillian McKeith is angry with me.   We fight.
You come out of it looking like the oldest drawing of a ghost in the world,
pass through the front door with ease, a black moon in the sky:

all crater   [citation needed]
I come out of this as if from a lift with a crowbar, vest top, glistening shoulders
[citation needed]
It's fine, I rewrite all of our history like this.

2

February and a pumpkin rolls off a table into your hands. We start again, seasonless,
enter a state of heavy moss all over
/the small opera of the domestic house
/lines of crossing and return
/more adjacence than anyone here can stand
/the mesh of a trolley, a grill
/the coolant pipes behind the refrigerator.

My main innovation at this time is to seal the element inside a metal tube and
place it in the same chamber as the water itself, a high-stakes game of truth or dare.

3

You flush along the jawline behind the glass panel of my front door all
forehead and fingers on the obscured surface   not frosted glass but
steam cleansing scattered dirt from the clavicle
citing

/large thrown stones
/the bones of your hip
/the entire underwater obstacle of the human skeleton

There are so many ways to paint this:
by numbers it's a long game cycling periods of activity with inactivity, I —
chew gum, doodle newspaper corners gothic, experiment with fuses, your attention.
I have heard there are people who instantly know

> which way an escalator is running or which way
> an arrow is pointing just by looking
> even though   an arrow is a device
> in which three times as many
> lines are pointing the wrong way.

4

There are phases in a child's development where they use words like *yesterday*
and *tomorrow* interchangeably
like the only thing that makes time directional

> is saying it. John asks *are we*
> *going to the beach yesterday?*

and I listen so hard I accidentally set the sound waves
> on fire
> and we watch them bounce around the room
> from surface to surface like starling**s in**
> murmuration across dry gra**ssland.**
> I put them out with **unboiled**

water, try to **hear**

proximately

knuckle down

and keep working on the design

for the kettle. The watched words

drift broken and

smoking toward us like

all the disappointing photos of the moon ever taken

[delicious fresh water] [citation needed]

5

I learn about other ways to make tea, run your lumpy plasma through

Mesopotamian vessels

experiment with spouts

and flow.

These are great

examples, my counsellor says, so I keep

going, adding to my list of places you still

are, things that helped:

/you locked out on our doorstep

/you two miles out to sea on a composite door

/you taking the night bus to the 24-hour McColls

/you as a water-damaged still in someone else's wallet [citation needed]

There is a whole lot of existence in the world to go around, there are

a whole lot of

finishes to choose from, matt or gloss, with a border or   without

plastic, jug-style, which is more efficient as one cup's worth covers the element

with

reference information[1]

---

1   Citation needed

6

During one of my experiments all the electric kettles in the
world boil at once—just once—and on that day no-one dies

    There are power outages from the electricity usage
     surge and we're in the dark drinking tea glowing full of   bones and past tenses.

I would do anything to follow you into the water table except do it.
Here's the breakthrough:

        Unstraighforward loss *flexes*
        (triggered by the rising steam as the water comes to boil
        thereby cutting off the current
        and the kettle switches off by itself.

7

I sell a heap of these and become a well-known millionaire.

Maxim Asks the Man

A man wearing a fossil badge knocks, selling G-d, so
Maxim asks the man/ *It's all lies,* the man says and I
wonder if I found a lie buried deep in the Earth what
kind of lie it would be and what it would take for me
to strap it to my chest.

Search History

Lou Reed loved raisins, you tell me fondly, it was in his rider. And David Bowie got through the seventies on red peppers, raw eggs and milk. We eliminate suspicion, visit friends where we can, continue stretching out our marriage until it is wide and low to the ground like uncooked pizza base. I vow never to google *Lou Reed* and *raisins* together, but one day I do it. It's like I clicked on a bad link: seconds apart you send me stock photos of Patti Smith eating a breakfast bap, Bowie with noodles, Ringo eating eggs in a red shirt, another of Lou Reed and a waiter, their hands buried deeply together, in that moment, in a heartfelt cortex of spaghetti. We fit underfloor heating to all the pavements in our district council area, turn it on, make pizza, stay married.

Jessica DMs Me a Photograph of Badly Decorated Eggs at Easter

It's a minute to three by the river & I am thinking about the categorisation of animals according to their misfortune: farm animals or zoo animals or caged hens. I phone the talking clock when I'm hungry & at the third pip we talk about how time can be either wild or domesticated, how it may be derived from the seed of an ancient grass-like species. The talking clock is not interested in the egg picture Jessica has sent me. The talking clock interrupts to say that time can be any temperature at all, but nothing is the same temperature as time & that is why the temperature of other things modulates: constantly warming or cooling. The whole universe. This must be monitored closely, which is why there are jam thermometers & weather presenters. Time is prepared differently by different cultures & becomes poisonous if it is allowed to cool too slowly. I hang up, still hungry as the receiver melts. It's not as if the river can desist from being swum in by labradors or stop itself from thinking about the grey tongues of giraffes. I eat that fat watch right off your wrist.

Haiku from the other side of the road

A swan flies low across the road
    Yes!   Show me your blunt teeth

When the Translator Is Grieving

Keeps thinking about the unrelated rubber burn to the
dead man's hand and not the genders
framing objects and abstract nouns
across Europe and
more distant, expensive languages at a price
greater than £150 per A4 sheet.

People respond on the forum with the grammatical
gender of death laid cold on the oldest
parts of the tongue:
                    In the Romance languages as it is for
                    Urdu, Hindi and Gujarati, it's female.

Some don't use masculine or feminine
at all but call things instead by animate or
inanimate determiners; some Slavic languages use both.
She looks at
Hungarian, Finnish, Estonian.

The man lay dead in a room with a cold fireplace
in a tongue where neither life nor fire were male
nor female, neither animate nor inanimate
and everything had abstracted itself without difficulty
from its recent state.

                    At the conference the translator's grief is abstract and
                    gaseous and does not enter the main lounge,
                    though she does and her lanyard confirms that she can.

When the translator is grieving she can no longer
absorb the untranslatable nuances broken
between languages and these come loose,
a kind of air- or paper-borne pollution.

> She recalls a paper about the Finnish verb 'kuulua' she read
> about eighteen months ago
> sometimes meaning 'to be perceptible (through hearing)'
> and its notional negative: to be imperceptible (through hearing).

The delegates' later reactions to the inexplicable
nuances present but undetectable in the subclauses
is hard to read, except by one another

> (*kuulua* is most often used with animate subjects.
> Here, the non-appearance of an animate being is heard but not
> perceived.)

The delegates agree never to meet again.

The translator keeps in her throat the whole day the most
violent and glottal words for the thing they say will help
though neither vaqt, цаг хугацаа nor Zeit are aggressive
enough in the mouth to refute that time

> is a good dog, travels well in the backs of cars
> does not swim in the corvid sea grease
> does not come to the door during a
> knock knock joke or a hurricane
> keeps its thoughts about former Yugoslavian oral poets to itself
> adores the givers of dinner along established lines of
> G-d, hero, object, a nice box of epithets.

Le poisson diseur de bonne aventure
is the French name for the Fortune Telling Fish
present in crackers at Christmastime.

Later into December, you stay busy moving your
head, tail, head and tail, curling your sides, turning over,
motionless, curling up entirely then

        one day, late at night
        you place your shoes to dry inches from the fire
        and hours later
        pick them up again.

Neil told me

it's best to cook mushrooms in threes said he read it in
Jamie Oliver but it was a strange joke which I enjoyed because it sounded
so plausible like being in love for a long time which back then
was still strange and made me hungry and because however long the world lasts
it is better to have three mushrooms than two

When Lindsay Denton from BBC TV Show Line of Duty *Pins a Man to the wall of a Multistorey Car Park by his Legs and Dew Forms on My Google Search for "In the Hopeless Expectation of Death" (Being an Oral or Written Statement by a Person on the Point of Death Concerning the Cause of their Death)*

In the mild expectation of hopeless peril
      of the woman at the car boot stall listing the different kinds of
      cancer available
         talking over tarpaulin selling LPs and shampoo
         and a half-used bottle of KY Jelly
In the hopeless expectation of crossing a major series in six weeks
         of inhaling water
         of heart attack
         of death
In the expectation, however hopeless, of spring
In the parting expectation of limbs
         mine and yours
In the dogged belief of the best of times and nothing else
In the total expectation of buying one and getting one free
         and still crossing the road with full care
In the naked expectation of not looking like I work here
         in the 50p orange T-shirt that everyone says looks like a uniform
         for any shop
         they've ever been in
In the hopeless, magnetic expectations of other planets
In the audacious, award-winning expectation of crowdfunding forests
         which is IVF for trees
         then clearing up afterwards
In the dreadful, rational lines between countries

In the heavy expectation of stolen fields
        and of falling in love
        with a life-adjacent experience
In the breath-filled expectation of waking parts
In the breathless expectation of a detailed inventory:
        79 snowdrops, handfulls of Palma violets by the canal
        of a penlight shining on the eye
        from one side
        to the other
        and back again
In the hopeless expectation of pieces of a face
        of a discredited supercomputer or sub-postmaster
        of a belt embedded in a woman
        of a wire fence embezzling a tree trunk
In the building expectation of a malfunctioning heatshield
In the endless expectation of a secret ice age
        between us
In the cropped-out expectation of geology
        a rock falls on a man
In the blacked-out expectation of the official document
In the hopeless expectation of meeting everyone else alive at the moment
        or just everyone called Lindsay
        and holding each other until the room is empty
        and all that's left of us is arms
In the meaningless exercise of taking an average of everybody called Lindsay
        at the moment
In the hopeless expectation of petrified forests
        abandoned petrol stations
        and other preserving features of landscape memory
In the hopeless expectation of a reversing vehicle
        a refundable whale
        of rising iron levels

and falling bin collections
In the hopeless expression on the face of a cartoon mascot
In the gradual expectation of a common language
    and the many understanding
    more than one
In the fading familiarity of my own hands
In the hopeless expectation of TV adverts for TVs
In the quantitative expectation of a second gunshot
    a second series
    a second horse
In the hopeless expectation of coming to at the end of a series
    or repeatedly on the same concrete steps
    or picking carrots in a field
    at 3 am
In the hopeless expectation of death in a multistorey car park
    then surviving anyway
In the hopeless realisation that the face getting older in other people's
    bathroom mirrors
    is my own
In the hopeless expectation of counting up all of the arrogance and
    all of the water required to live
    but running out of measuring cylinders
In the hopeless expectation of breath condensing into water
    and the breathless expectation of arrogance condensing into night
    from vapor
    to dew
    as the temperature drops and the new object cools down

On Becoming Unwell After Reading a Biography of Richard III

When I was haunted by a fifteenth century king
and I mean I satin my bathroom and really worried about it for hours
and became afraid in that way that biblical characters are afraid:
of smiting and the earliest cliches of fruit, etc., having never known
the full pleasure of kitchen units, etc.
And I kicked the toothbrush holder and a hairbrush onto the floor
in shock, took from my pocket a burgundy notebook kept for spellings
where I tried to write his name carefully, but couldn't remember
the right numeral to end it. The king got things wrong too: kept
meaning to get going with the haunting but, of course, got transfixed
by things like the plumbing and the toaster and the whoopie cushions
in the small hands of my sons. I kept a diary of all the incidents like the
police say you should. I wrote *The king is not really alert, which is*
lucky for me. I suppose the haunting was just not that extravagant.
I tried to rest but really just performed it in the way I have picked up
over the years from advertising: I wrote sleepsleepsleep
on all the A frame boards of the main street and climbed into the
oversized armchairs of 90s anticongestant commercials, now preserved
only between stretches of film on videotape joining together all those
who recorded it at the time of transmission.
I pretend to sleep but instead search for Amazon reviews of Richard III
when he is not looking. One man found his experience *very enlightening,*
professionally carried out, funny and very much worthwhile, while
another complained that Richard III just kept *turning away and*
putting his hand in his mouth. I guess my experience was somewhere
in the middle: Three stars: A vase full of sunflowers going mad
in a north-facing room. You can name a star after someone
but the black holes are all spoken for. The king is
rubbing his eyes and acting blasé about having a body again and I'm

biting the side of my hand until the skin changes shape.

I imagine my troubles as a videorecorder full of bees, jam open the door so they can all flyaway like princes from a tower; the lonely price of gold. The videotape of the anticongestant commercial becomes covered in honey which is unwatchable but on-brand. I try to spread the blame for everything. One day when I am feeling a little better, I explain to the king that all the whoopie cushions ever made will rot away, the rubber, the foam and the tiny metal ring all coming apart towards forever loudly, the kings, the scraps of thought, millions of impressions of day and night, day and night, the video recorder, all of it crowded together in the same SPAR shop car park, the same Soviet bus station, the same small lift, travelling upwards through the vertical space of a department store containing literally everything, all shooting into the sun at once saying *here I am*. This happens right near the end of the haunting and is the only time I get a reaction out of him. *I'm done with this*, he says, and I apologise, but not extravagantly, and I'm better, but not forever.

This Recovery Doesn't Fit

like a helicopter introduced into a residential building
        no this isn't a list of things that won't fit
next I say you make me want to screenshot all the instances of
extras looking right at the camera and swear
that this is just about qualities   anything not green is
painted to look green while bystanders
produce perfect casts of their insides over and over
it makes me laugh abnormally and I mean like
from the inside of a Rachel Whiteread house
        in the kitchen I tilt all the spotlights down   pretend
gravity has taken hold over light and claim it was me
who invented black holes
        the air crash investigator has great hair and anyway
tell me a thing that doesn't happen dangerously close
to the ground?

Partial Biography with Chital Deer

The tiger low in the grass, the deer loose chewing
it's all rods and cones, the way the orange is green, the way
the tiger is coming this way unseen through gold-
green curtains so unfashionable in living rooms just now
through the long grass of former lovers and glossy interior spreads
the wronged woman running like an unlisted ingredient through cake mix
thinking about: greenhouse glass, summer straps, the company of strangers.
I don't know, what's comforting?

had all the organs in her body transform one by one into objects of the home this was not a feminist comment but a progressive disease her ovaries twin bookends kept soft tissue on the shelf her liver bent into a soup tin pop art for the radiographers' pleasure alone she manages to live life pretty normally at first takes the bus without too much clanking/ unpleasantness enjoys old James Bond movies through tooth-ache pills on slow afternoons achieves minor celebrity and the impression of respect as a generous punchline among MRI technicians and airport workers but fails to become as famous as you'd think: *Take-a-Break* and *The Hollywood Enquirer* of course say yes perfect more while members of the hospital's PR department talk sternly over lunch, ask *is this what we call news now?* she makes a modest living travelling between fetes with a 40 cm square trestle table and has a semi-permanent display board at the Museum of the Home/ looks normal displays outrageous x-rays is accused of putting feminism back 50 years with her Tupperware gall bladder and showy lack of any serious organs at all she is a popular guest on daytime chat shows until one morning on that false couch someone calls in with the knowing-something-you-don't-know intonation of what she'd call (and does) *a right wanker*, the light from the studio playing her face like Tuesday morning biology thirty-five years ago the first time she'd learnt from a man that the skin is an organ too at a Formica desk fake wood by the cavity wall legs flinch from the heating pipe melting chocolate bars in her pocket already the rustle of tin foil but not yet the glint/ *it's the largest one you know*/ the realisation brings her out in a thick overbearing sweat but the foil is impermeable sealed around her cuticles like the seams on showroom tents as fast as climate change she expands and bursts on live TV like Violet Beauregard, the oven clock they use to this day for cooking demonstrations rumoured to be her hypertrophic heart where it landed.

Diatomite or Diatomaceous Earth or Moler Earth or Kieselguhr

In which I read a dictionary of building terms during your wedding

I am a good friend; I do not lick the salt emerging from
the cheap bricks of new cul-de-sacs like a horse might.
I do not

       name them for the varieties of tree they have
replaced or the horses they tilted their spines towards in the
hot weather.

       I apologise for being arrogant, at times furious
about the names of native trees about which I know
very little.

       I consider economies of scale when building a lot of
houses all at once. I do not name it but I learn the number
which represents

       love's coefficient of expansion. I hear it small and repeating
in the hollow siliceous skeletons of tiny marine and freshwater
organisms

       and also between the crackers of the cheese trolly.
Bricks made of love float on water. I do not name the water.
I do not drink it.

       Love acts as an absorbent for the nitroglycerin in dynamite.
I apologise for the patient difference between alkalines, which is
really not my fault.

You accept my apology. Different subject new line turns
your heart from a pumping station into a wedding venue bunting
the aorta hard,

regardless of papers published by cardiac surgeons. Talking
to you here is like phoning a golden eagle and asking: where are
the toilets please?

or semaphoring a council official to their face. There's dancing.
Something in the kitchen sets the alarm: just three beeps. I checked
online and it's OK

to put out fire with water that's already hot. It's quite a material
it has a lot of names: diatomite or diatomaceous earth or moler earth
or Kieselguhr.

And you know, I got married first.

If Something Has Fallen into the Box by Mistake You Have a Week's Grace to Find It

After Sir Patrick Moore's Obituary of Fellow Astronomer Reg Spry

Chapter 1: Sight

Patrick Moore states that Reg Spry was born within sight of the Greenwich Observatory, whose Great Equatorial Telescope sees galaxies millions of light years away but could not have observed the birth of the late amateur astronomer, whose own eyesight was quoted by Moore as being "not good."

> **Perspective**
>
> i) A newborn baby can see approximately the distance of its mother's face when held to the breast.
>
> ii) The Great Equatorial Telescope turns like a man in a neck brace, but the birth of Reg Spry (1902) remains blurred and obscure.

Chapter 2: Obscura

Sitting next to the earth where we buried my dog, after returning from the pub, 12:30 am. Light arrives, having been given millions enough light years of notice but stops at the surface of the soil: cattle grid for something holy, obscurer of the precise. When an object is moving towards us, its light moves towards the blue end of the spectrum as its wavelengths get shorter. This is called blue shift.

The Great Equatorial Telescope does not see the lunch of Reg Spry as he prepares it that day in 1990 (Moore states that Spry was preparing for lunch when he suddenly collapsed and died of a heart attack).

> **Perspective**
>
> i) My starting point for this poem was "What is not within sight of Greenwich Observatory?"

ii) For this poem I asked the Royal Observatory on Twitter how far their telescope could see. *Telescopes don't really have a limit on how far they can see,* they said, *just how faint an object they can see.*

Chapter 3: Output

Spry wrote a book called *Make Your Own Telescope From Everyday Materials* (Sigwell & Jackson Ltd., 1978). I have one of the results in my attic, a foolish darkness to ask of a telescope. I keep meaning to concrete it to my yard.

Spry is dead within sight of snooker breaks in the twenties and thirties, mastery of all those coloured balls and calmly, says Patrick, so calmly despite three real tragedies and the very respectable playing of a piano, repairing radio masts on a precarious ledge hundreds of feet up.

Perspective

i) I inherited this book suddenly in the middle of a November night, my father's wavelengths going long long long.

ii) My father's last instructions were eight words long; over the next six months I found many duplicates of these words in his room.

iii) The last eight words of *Make Your Own Telescope From Everyday Materials* are: "you have a week's grace to find it."

Acknowledgements

'Call for Help' was first published in *Peach Mag* (March 2021).

'Carotid Artery I Can Hear the Sea' was first published in issue 22 of *SAND* (February 2021).

'During or After a Party' was first published in issue 9 of *Paris Lit Up* (date TBC).

'Following Advice to Be Myself at a Party [with subtitles]' was first published in *bath magg* (December 2020).

'Fossdyke and the Native Speed of Birds' was first published in the Anthropocene issue of *Magma* (#81) (October 2021).

'Futility of Trying to Enter a 240-Year-Old Public House from Orbit' was first published in the spring edition of *The Rialto* (June 2021).

'Neil told me' was first published in *Potluck Zine x SPOONFEED* (October 2021).

'Palm Pocket Palm' was first published in *Stand* (Autumn 2022).

'Unusable Tarot Reading from the Passenger Seat of a Crashed Peugeot 205 (1997)' was first published in *Booth* (May 2023).

An earlier version of 'What Keeps Me Going Is' was published in the Bad Betty Press anthology *The Book of Bad Betties* (September 2021).

'When I Was a Hammerhead Shark' and 'People Just Add Something; This Time the Thing Is a Mole' were first published in *Granta* (December 2022).

You Do Know was first published in the anthology *Bi+ Lines*, ed. Helen Bowell (fourteen poems, 2023)

Thanks to Maxim, Bill, Arthur, Rufus and John. My mum. My dad, even though he is dead. To Aaron and the folks at Broken Sleep for saying yes, and for all the good work they do. To Eamonn, Nikki, Rachel, TonyBob, Ollie, Lorraine and families. To Mark. To Liz (yellow car!) and Georgie for always saying something in a poem. To Becci & Mark, Matt & Kate, Roxy, Chris, Suzi, Joe, Kirsty, Julia, Neil (from 'Neil Told Me'), Massimo, Steve. To people called Etty and Babb. To Josephine, Michael, all the McKinnells and Dina and the Foxes and everyone I've forgotten to mention by name. To Sue, Frances, Cate, Hannah, Sam and families. To Gershon Silins for being the rabbi in 'You do Know' and to Josephine Westlake for being the geographer in the same. To my amazing students (just wow), my friends at LJC, my drag king friends, my friends at SO Festival. To Megan and my friends at Versal, to Dan and my friends at the University of Lincoln—impossible to quantify how much I owe them. To Jimmy, who was shocked to be thanked in my first book because he totally underestimates the importance in my life of him running into my room that time in 1999 after reading a bunch of my late teenage poems. Look, I thanked you again! To Rachel, Flower, Greeny et al. We had a good time at that old place! To cris. to Jerome: thanks. To Ian Timson who I rode at the top of the bus with and is missed every day in this town. To the amazing folk at the bus station who work hard to get me home when I'm playing second wheelchair on the last bus. To Katy Flippance, Jean Sadler, that guy with long hair whose name I can't remember, and everyone else who helped me with my mental health over the years. Really.

No thanks to the bus companies whose buses only have one wheelchair space and no plans to change that. No thanks. Not really.

LAY OUT YOUR UNREST